INTERACT

Plane Crazy

Richard Cooper

SERIES CONSULTANT: LORRAINE PETERSEN

RISING STARS

nasen
Helping Everyone Achieve

NASEN House, 4/5 Amber Business Village, Amber Close, Amington,
Tamworth, Staffordshire B77 4RP

Rising Stars UK Ltd.
22 Grafton Street, London W1S 4EX
www.risingstars-uk.com

Text © Rising Stars UK Ltd.

The right of Richard Cooper to be identified as the author of this work has been asserted by him in accordance with the Copyright, Design and Patents Act 1998.

Published 2009

Cover design: Burville-Riley Partnership
Illustrator: Dave Neale for Advocate Art
Text design and typesetting: Andy Wilson for Green Desert Ltd.
Publisher: Gill Budgell
Editor: Catherine Gilhooly
Series consultant: Lorraine Petersen

All rights reserved. No part of this publication may be reproduced, stored in a retrieval system, or transmitted in any form by any means, electronic, mechanical, photocopying, recording or otherwise without the prior permission of Rising Stars UK Ltd.

British Library Cataloguing in Publication Data.
A CIP record for this book is available from the British Library

ISBN 978-1-84680-499-1

Printed by Craft Print International Limited, Singapore

Contents

Characters	4
Scene 1: **After school**	7
Scene 2: **Online at FaceSpace**	15
Scene 3: **In the playground**	27
Scene 4: **Game over!**	37
In the chatroom ...	46

Characters

Solly
Solly loves making things but he finds it difficult to make friends.

Emma
Solly's older sister. She thinks Solly is a geek.

Kate
A friend of Emma. She makes an effort to get to know Solly.

Characters

Alfie
Alfie is in Emma's class. He loves going on the Internet to keep in touch with everyone he knows.

Daryl
A friend of Emma. He thinks it's cool that Solly has a talent for design and technology.

Narrator
The narrator tells the story.

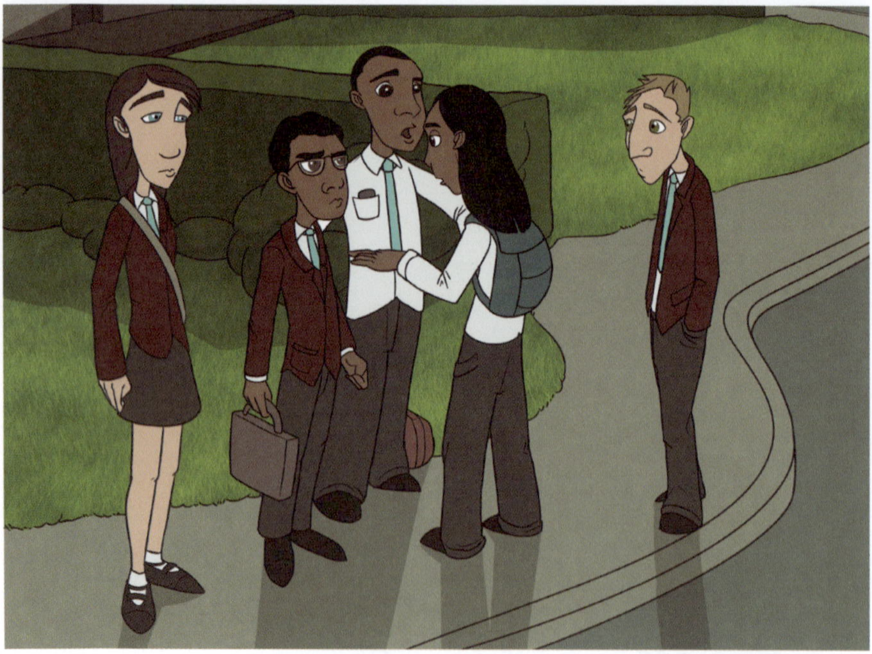

Scene 1
AFTER SCHOOL

Narrator Solly has won a big competition by building a model aeroplane. This means he gets to fly his plane at the Paris Air Show. He has been praised by the head teacher in front of the whole school.

Alfie Hey, Emma, there's your brother.

Daryl He did really well to win that competition. We don't see him around much, though.

Plane Crazy

Emma He's such a geek! He's been out of school for a few terms.

Alfie Why hasn't he been in school?

Emma He didn't get on with the kids or the teachers. Mum and Dad have been teaching him at home.

Kate Let's call him over. Solly, over here!

Solly I'll walk on my own, thanks.

Narrator Solly lifts up his collar and tries to ignore them all.

Daryl Lucky guy, no school!

Kate Pretty lonely though. No friends to talk to.

Solly I do have some friends, thank you very much.

Scene 1   After school

Narrator	Alfie, Daryl and Kate try to get to know Solly a bit better as they walk home.

Alfie   Loved the model plane, Solly.

Daryl   Yeah, I bet you could make anything.

Solly   Thanks guys but …

Kate   But what? You've won a trip to Paris – that's wicked!

Solly   I know, it's great, but I don't want people to make a fuss.

Emma   That's right. You don't want to get too big for your boots do you? Mum and Dad can't afford to pay for you to go to Paris anyway.

Solly   I know. I'll have to get a part-time job. The prize was just to go on to the next part of the competition in Paris. It didn't include getting there!

Plane Crazy

Alfie How much does a ticket to Paris cost?

Solly I don't know yet.
I'll find out on the Internet.

Daryl Are you going by ferry, train or plane?

Emma Plane, of course. He's just built
an aeroplane – he can go in that!

Solly Whatever is cheapest, I guess.

Narrator The group are checking their phones
for messages and chatting.

Alfie Hey Solly, text me your number.
I'll add you to my address book.

Solly Err, thanks Alfie. Here you go.

Kate Give your number to anyone
do you, Solly?
I'd be more careful.

Scene 1 After school

Emma Solly needs all the friends he can get.
You should see his FaceSpace page.
'Billy No Mates'!

Daryl You're on FaceSpace?
Me too! I'll look you up.

Narrator The group start talking about the new FaceSpace website.

Alfie My home page is brilliant!
You should see some of the photos.

Kate Yeah, but can you take down that one of me dressed as Shrek!

Daryl It was a fancy-dress party.
I went as a gorilla.

Emma Yeah, when are you going to take the suit off?

Solly Hey, Emma. Why do you always have to wind people up?

Plane Crazy

Narrator Emma and Solly start to argue.
Daryl stops them.

Daryl Relax, guys. Emma was only teasing.
I can take it.

Emma See why he was out of school?
He's my brother but he's such a pain!

Kate Most younger brothers are, Emma.
There's no need to be so unkind.

Solly She hates me and I hate her.

Alfie Emma should be pleased for you.

Narrator The group start to joke about
all going to Paris.

Kate I'd love to go. All those French boys!

Daryl Huh! Don't they eat snails and things
like that over there?

Emma Solly should eat snails – he needs to
come out of his shell!

Scene 1   After school

Solly   Leave it Emma, before I …

Alfie   Look, chill guys. Solly is going to Paris and we're not. Simple.

Narrator   The group start to go their separate ways home.

Daryl   See you all later. Oh, and you too Solly.

Alfie   I bet Solly is going home to brush up on his French phrases!

Kate   I hope you get the money to go to Paris, Solly. Bye!

Narrator   Emma turns to her brother.

Emma   Come on, I've had enough of you embarrassing me in front of my friends.

Solly   You can do that well enough by yourself. Just leave me alone will you?

Narrator	Emma and Solly go home one way. The others go in a different direction.

Alfie That Solly is a bit of a boffin.
I've seen him a few times making stuff
in the tech room with Mr Sykes.

Kate It must be hard for him to start back
at school again after all this time.

Daryl I know, let's all nudge him on FaceSpace
tonight. Show him he's got some mates.

Narrator	Meanwhile, Emma and Solly are still arguing.

Emma I suppose you're locking yourself away
in your room when we get home.
All you do is work on that stupid plane.

Solly Yes, it keeps me well away from you!

Scene 2

Online at FaceSpace

Narrator	Solly gets home and works on his model plane. Later he logs on to his FaceSpace home page. His sister's friends have logged on too, but they are using their FaceSpace user names. Solly doesn't realise who they are.
Solly	Hey, I've got mail. That's unusual.
Narrator	Solly starts to type.
Solly	'Hello, who's this?'

Plane Crazy

Kate 'Welcome aboard, Solly.
I love those pictures of your planes.'

Alfie 'Me too. Can I add you to my list of FaceMates?'

Daryl 'I can't believe you made those planes yourself. Add me to your list of mates too.'

Narrator Somebody else joins in the online chat, with the user name Sykeo. Sykeo types, *'Well I think it's sad really, but whatever.'* Solly and his four new 'friends' start to chat in the FaceSpace chatroom.

Solly 'Who are you? How did you find my home page?'

Scene 2   Online at FaceSpace

Alfie   'You go to my school. I look up everyone there on FaceSpace.'

Kate   'Yeah, the Internet hides some weird stuff and weird people, man!'

Daryl   'Solly, you should have a user name to hide who you are.'

Narrator   Sykeo types, '*You don't want the whole world to know all your secrets, do you?*' Solly is a bit nervous. He's never had anyone contact him through FaceSpace before, but he carries on.

Solly   'Well, I'm glad you like my planes. This one has won a competition.'

Daryl   'Well, I can see why, it's great.'

Kate   'Yeah, like me!'

Plane Crazy

Narrator	Sykeo types, '*Well now. Is that how you spend your spare time? Playing with toy aeroplanes?*'

Alfie	'That's not playing, that's real skill.'

Narrator	Solly's mum calls Solly and Emma down for tea. Afterwards they both go back to their computers.

Solly   'Are you guys still there?'

Kate   'I'm still here, Solly. Sykeo went offline for a while.'

Alfie   'Solly, that video you posted. Is that your plane?'

Scene 2   Online at FaceSpace

Solly   'Yep, that's my plane.'

Daryl   'Cool! It's doing some crazy tricks!'

Narrator   Sykeo returns to the chatroom.
He types, *'I'm back guys. Are you still looking at toy planes?'*
The time goes quickly as Solly explains more about his hobby.

Solly   'I need to raise some money so I can go to Paris for the next part of the competition.'

Alfie   'You will have to get a part-time job.'

Narrator   Sykeo makes a suggestion.
'Why not sell some of your toys at the teddy bears' picnic? You might raise 50p!'

Daryl   'Lay off him, Sykeo. You're just jealous. Bet you can't make anything like that.'

Plane Crazy

Kate   'I could make a plane, but it wouldn't be as good as Solly's!'

Narrator   It's getting late and Solly's mum calls for him to go to bed.

Solly   'I have to go now.
I've got to go to bed.'

Kate   'Well, good luck, Solly. I hope you can raise the money for your trip.'

Narrator   Sykeo types the message, *'Ah, bedtime for the little man. Sweet dreams airhead!'*

Alfie   'Ignore Sykeo. He doesn't know what he's saying.'

Daryl   'I'm your friend Solly. Tell Sykeo to get lost!'

Scene 2 Online at FaceSpace

Narrator Solly logs off and goes to bed.
Later in the night he wakes up
and sees his computer is still on.
He turns it off and goes back to sleep.
The next morning he logs on to his
FaceSpace home page.

Solly Oh no! My home page!
What's happened?

Narrator Sykeo is online too.
'Hello Solly, nice photos!'

Plane Crazy

Kate   'Is that really you in the pictures, Solly?'

Alfie   'Yeah, pictures of you as a baby
with a dummy in your mouth!'

Daryl   'Why did you post those pictures, Solly?
... Solly, are you there?'

Narrator   Solly is too upset to go to school.
He sees his sister Emma leaving
the house.

Solly   I can't go back to school again.
Everyone will have seen my baby photos.
I bet it was you, Emma!

Emma   Oh well, just like old times.
I'll go to school on my own then.

Narrator   Emma leaves Solly at home.
She catches up with her friends
on the way to school.

Emma   Hey guys, wait for me!

Scene 2   Online at FaceSpace

Alfie   Hi Emma, where's your brother?

Daryl   Yeah, we had a wicked chat last night about his planes. But someone called Sykeo was well out of order.

Kate   Is Solly coming in today? My dad said he would give him a part-time job in his cafe.

Emma   Solly is crying about those photos on his home page.

Alfie   You mean he didn't put them up?

Daryl   Come on Alfie, what do you think?

Kate   Someone else must have been on his computer and uploaded the pictures … Emma, it wasn't you, was it?

Emma   No!

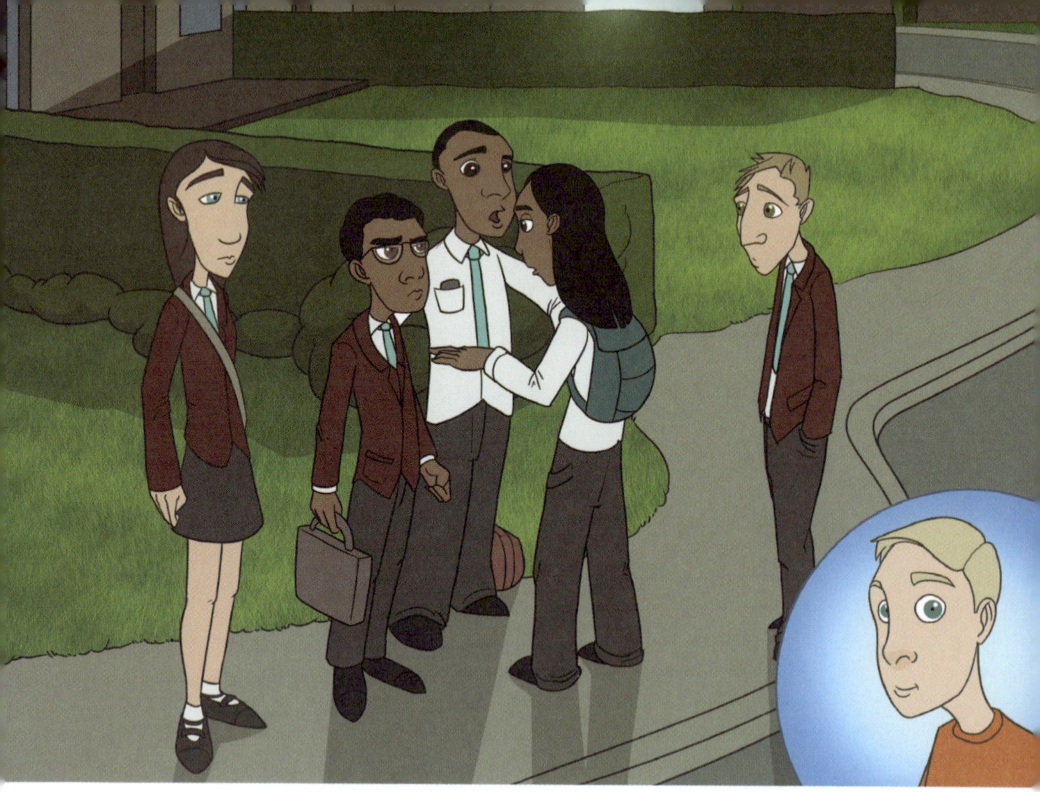
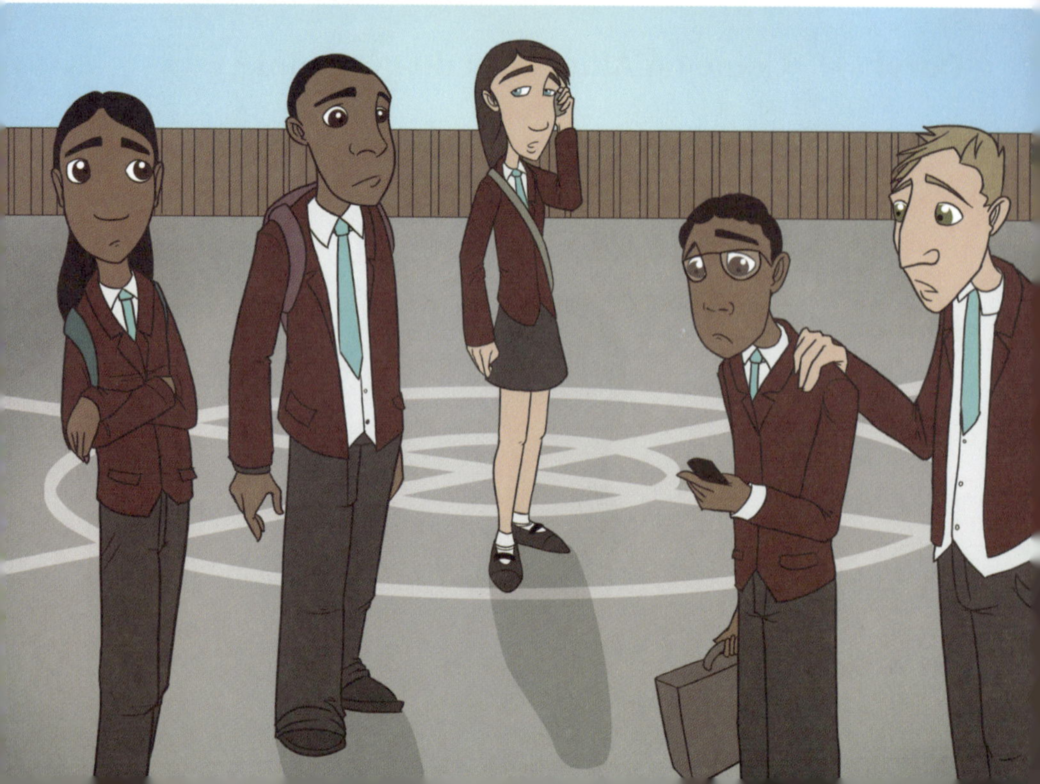

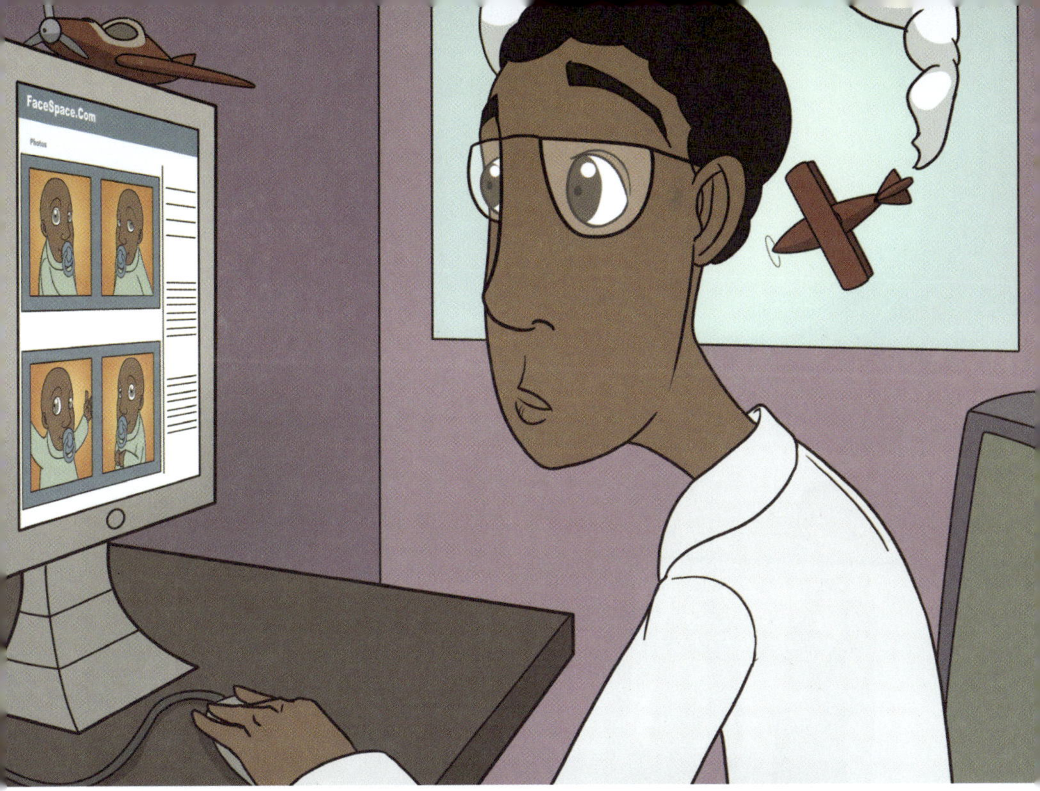
FaceSpace.Com
Photos

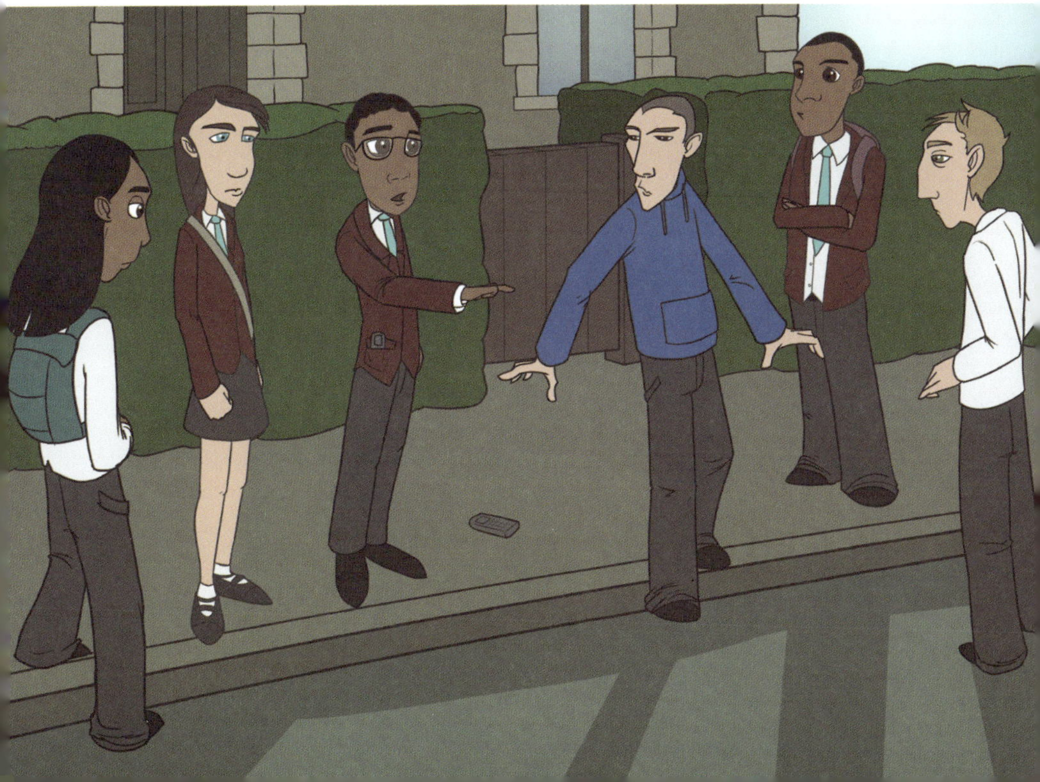

Plane Crazy

Scene 3

IN THE PLAYGROUND

Narrator The group are talking about what has happened to Solly's home page.

Alfie Emma, I think you did put those pictures up on Solly's home page. You were really nasty to him yesterday.

Emma We might not get on but I would never do a horrible thing like that to him!

Daryl Emma, have you changed your user name on FaceSpace? It wouldn't be Sykeo would it?

Plane Crazy

Kate Hey, look who's coming through the gate. It's Solly!

Solly Hi guys. I'm really sorry Emma, I owe you an apology.

Narrator The group gather round Solly to hear what has happened.

Solly Those pictures. They were put on my home page by my mum.

Daryl No way! Why did she do that?

Kate She can't have done it on purpose!

Emma Our mum is hopeless with computers.

Alfie But what was she doing on FaceSpace in the first place?

Scene 3   In the playground

Narrator   Solly explains that while he was asleep, his mum came into his room to use his computer.

Solly   Mum wanted to send some baby photos of me to our auntie in Australia.

Emma   I get it. Her photos are stored on Solly's computer.

Kate   She must have uploaded the ones she wanted and left the others open.

Alfie   And then she must have downloaded them to your home page by mistake. Nightmare!

Narrator   They all feel sorry for Solly and tell him they'll look out for him. Solly has deleted all the baby photos from his home page.

Kate   So, who is this Sykeo then? I really thought it was you, Emma.

Plane Crazy

Emma No way. I was doing my homework last night. Anyway, my user name is still 'The Princess'.

Solly Whoever Sykeo is, I don't want to hear from him again.

Narrator School ends and the group head for Kate's dad's cafe. They sit down and have some cake and drinks.

Kate My dad says he'll pay you to make sandwiches for the cafe after school. Four pounds an hour.

Solly That's great! I can earn enough money for my trip to Paris.

Scene 3   In the playground

Emma Oh well, at least you'll be out after school and I can watch the TV in peace!

Alfie Hey, come on, Solly's with us now.

Daryl Yeah, I want a go at flying his plane!

Kate Emma's only joking … I hope. Come on Solly, drink up. My dad will show you what to do.

Narrator Solly learns how to make sandwiches and starts his new after-school job. A few days later the group are walking to school together.

Daryl How much do you have for your trip now, Solly?

Solly Forty pounds. Another couple of weeks and I'll have enough money for my plane ticket!

Kate How exciting! Flying to Paris!

Alfie This competition you won …
who entered it?

Emma It was a big competition.
Solly beat everyone in his age group.
It was really hard.

Narrator Just then, Solly gets a text message.

Daryl Who's that, Solly?

Emma Yeah, who's it from? We're the only ones in your address book and it's not from any of us!

Kate Look at his face … something's wrong.

Alfie Solly, you've gone very pale.
What is it?

Solly It's from the competition people.
The Paris Air Show has been cancelled!

Scene 3   In the playground

Narrator   They all read Solly's text.

Daryl   It must be a mistake, Solly. Don't worry.

Emma   I'll call the number and find out.

Alfie   The number's blocked.
I've tried it already.

Kate   Okay, I'll get the number.

'Hello? Yes, I want the number for the Paris Air Show please. Yes, put me through, thank you.'

Narrator	They all wait nervously while Kate is on the phone.

Solly   Well, what do they say?

Kate   The show is going ahead as planned.
They don't know anything about it
being cancelled.
And they didn't call you.

Daryl   Someone is playing nasty games here.
Who would do that?

Emma   Someone who wants to get at Solly.

Alfie   Who would want to hurt him?
He's harmless!

Kate   Of course, but he must have upset
someone.

Solly   I just want to fly my planes.
How can that upset anyone?

Scene 3   In the playground

Narrator   The group try and think who might be cyber-bullying Solly.

Daryl   What about the competition you won ... who came second?

Solly   Well, Mr Sykes was working on a plane too. You know – the tech guy at school.

Alfie   Hmm. I think we may have a suspect!

Kate   Mr Sykes? Surely not!

Plane Crazy

Scene 4
GAME OVER!

Narrator The group meet up again after school and head towards the cafe.

Daryl I'm going to have one of your sandwiches Solly.
I'm really hungry today!

Emma Me too. Cheese and ham on brown bread for me.

Solly Can I recommend the tuna and sweetcorn?

Alfie That will do me, mate!

Plane Crazy

Kate   Hold on, my dad's just sent me a text. He wants to see Solly right now.

Narrator   Solly gets a text from Kate's dad as well. When they all get to the cafe, Kate's dad tells Solly he is sacked.

Solly   That's it. I'll never get to Paris now.

Kate   Why did my dad sack you? He looked really cross!

Alfie   Yeah, he was waving something around. It looked like a tuna sandwich.

Emma   I heard him say the words 'food poisoning'.

Daryl   Perhaps Solly has poisoned the customers!

Scene 4 Game over!

Narrator	Solly explains that there have been 20 complaints about the tuna sandwiches. Three people have been taken to hospital with food poisoning.
Solly	He said he got 18 complaints by text and two phone calls.
Daryl	There is something fishy about all this.
Alfie	Yes, the tuna!
Emma	Why don't we check with the hospital?
Kate	I'll call and see if anyone is ill after eating at Dad's cafe.
Narrator	Kate calls the hospital. No one has been there with food poisoning in the last few days.
Kate	Don't worry Solly, you'll get your job back.

Plane Crazy

Daryl First, let's work out who is behind this.

Emma What about Mr Sykes, the tech guy at school?

Alfie Sykes! The user name Sykeo was on FaceSpace the other night!

Narrator The kids all look at each other in surprise. They've just made the link between the names Sykes and Sykeo.

Solly I can't believe Mr Sykes would do anything like this. He's really helped me with my designs and stuff.

Scene 4 Game over!

Daryl Okay then, how about Mr Sykes's son, Eric? He goes to our school and he's a really mean bully.

Solly So ... maybe it's been Eric all along?

Kate I know where Eric lives.
Let's pay him a visit.

Solly Careful, we don't want any trouble.

Alfie Don't worry, I have a plan!

Emma Now where have I heard that before?

Narrator They go round to Eric's house and wait behind a hedge.

Alfie Okay, I've got Eric's mobile number. I'm going to send him some text messages from Solly's phone.

Kate Tell him that Solly isn't going to Paris now.

Emma Yeah, and there's a spare ticket and a place in the competition ...

Daryl And if he wants it, he must meet Solly outside in five minutes.

Solly Cool! That *is* a good plan.

Narrator Alfie sends the message. They all wait for the front door to open.
After five minutes, Eric comes out.

Emma Here he comes, quiet everyone.

Daryl He's holding his phone.
Look, he's sending a text message.

Solly My phone has just buzzed.
The message must be from him!

Kate He hasn't put a block on his number.
He's given himself away!

Alfie Right, get him, everyone!

Scene 4 Game over!

Narrator They all jump out from behind the hedge and surround Eric. Eric drops his phone on the floor in surprise.

Emma Right you, let's check your call log.

Kate Here we go! There are loads of calls and messages sent to my dad with today's date!

Solly And one sent to me yesterday. The one about the Air Show being cancelled.

Alfie Why you …

Daryl Easy, Alfie. Now we have all the proof we need.

Plane Crazy

Narrator   Eric confesses to having cyber-bullied Solly. He says he is sorry and promises to leave Solly alone.

Daryl   Eric thought that if Solly didn't go to Paris, then he could take his place. He would use the plane he worked on with his dad.

Emma   He tried all the dirty tricks in the book.

Kate   Well, he won't do anything like that again. And I'll make sure my dad gives Solly his job back.

Solly   I really hope he will … but I don't want to make any more tuna sandwiches for a while!

Alfie   Well, nothing can stop Solly now. Let's hope you and your plane can win an even bigger prize in Paris.

Scene 4   Game over!

Narrator	A month later, after the Air Show, the group all meet up at the cafe.

Daryl   Well, Solly, what happened?

Alfie   Yeah, did you win?

Emma   I've kept your secret safe, Solly ...

Kate   Of course he won. Look at his face!

Solly   A gold medal for flying skills, and a cup for the best model plane. You can see all the photos on my FaceSpace page!

In the chatroom ...

> You log onto FaceSpace and see Sykeo giving someone else a hard time.

FaceSpace

User Name: Sykeo

Adam, you are such a geek! I've seen those pictures of you in the school choir ... really sad!
Boys aren't meant to be good at singing. Why don't you join a sports team?
I know why ... You'd be rubbish, loser!

- How do you think Adam feels when he reads this message?
- What message could you post to support Adam and to try to stop Sykeo from cyber-bullying?

In pairs ...

One person takes the part of Solly, and the other person is Sykeo.

- Look back at the nasty things Sykeo has done, e.g. making fun of Solly and his hobby in Scene 2, and making Solly lose his job in Scene 4.
- Solly has to ask Sykeo questions about why he is being a bully.
- Can Sykeo explain his bad behaviour?
- Will he say sorry?

Tip: Think about times you have been jealous of somebody else. Did you support them, or did you pick on them to try and make yourself look stronger?

Pass it on ...

- *In small groups, think about an activity or a hobby that you really enjoy or are really good at.*
- *Take it in turns to tell each other about the hobby and why you enjoy it so much.*
- *After each turn, the other people in the group can ask you questions about your hobby.*

Tip: Show an interest in each other's hobbies. Try to praise other people in the group for what they are good at.

INTERACT

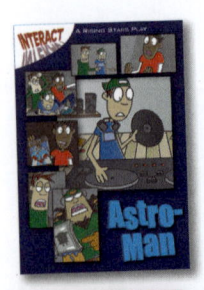

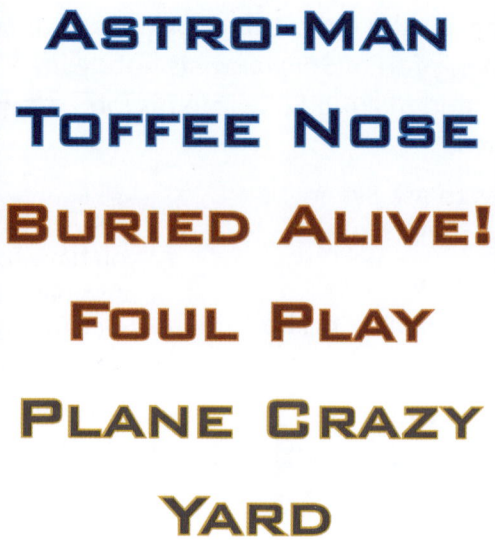

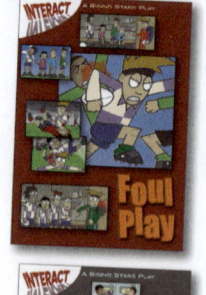

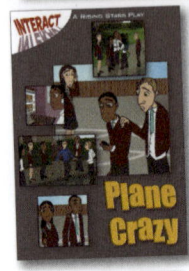

ASTRO-MAN

TOFFEE NOSE

BURIED ALIVE!

FOUL PLAY

PLANE CRAZY

YARD

DUMPED!

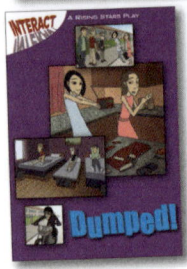

STEP WARS

Interact plays are available from booksellers or www.risingstars-uk.com

For more information please call 0800 091 1602

RISING ★ STARS